YOU Choose

Chin Up, Charlie

Be Brave

Sarah Eason

It might be useful for parents or teachers to read our 'How to use this book' guide on pages 28–29 before looking at Charlie's dilemmas. The points for discussion on these pages are helpful to share with your child once you have read the book together.

First published in 2011 by Wayland

Copyright © Wayland 2011

Wayland
338 Euston Road
London NW1 3BH

Wayland Australia
Level 17/207 Kent Street
Sydney, NSW 2000

Produced for Wayland by Calcium
Design: Paul Myerscough
Editor for Wayland: Camilla Lloyd
Illustrations by Ailie Busby

British Library Cataloguing in Publication Data

Eason, Sarah.
    Chin up, Charlie! Be brave.—(You choose!)
    1. Courage—Juvenile literature. 2. Courage—Juvenile fiction.
    I. Title II. Series
    179.6–dc22

ISBN: 978 0 7502 6642 0

Printed in China

Wayland is a division of Hachette Children's Books,
an Hachette UK company.
www.hachette.co.uk

Contents

Hello, Charlie!

Charlie is like a lot of children. He has some friends and is happy. But there are times when he gets **scared**, even though he wants to be **brave**.

Sometimes, you have to put your chin up and be brave. Follow Charlie as he finds himself in tricky situations in which he must choose to be **brave**.

YOU choose too!

Join in, Charlie

Charlie is feeling **shy** on his first day at school.

At break time, Charlie doesn't know if anyone will want to play with him. Sam asks him if he wants to play football.

What should Charlie choose to do?

Should Charlie:

a pretend he hasn't heard Sam?

b tell Sam he doesn't like football?

c smile and kick the ball to Sam?

Charlie, choose **c**

Don't be shy! It's fun making new friends. Someone you meet today might be your best friend before long. And everyone likes **friendly** people to play with.

What would **you** choose to do?

Go, Charlie

Rory has **invited** Charlie to
a **sleepover** at his house.

Charlie is **afraid** of the dark and doesn't want to go.

What should Charlie choose to do?

Should Charlie:

a tell Rory he can't come?

b take his night-light to Rory's so he can see in the dark?

c tell Rory to invite someone else instead?

Charlie, choose **b**

Don't worry, lots of people are scared of the dark. Rory will think having a night-light is cool! Sleepovers are too much fun to miss.

What would **YOU** choose to do?

Don't worry, Charlie

Charlie is going to the dentist and he is **scared**.

Mum says it's only a **check-up** and it won't hurt, but Charlie is still **frightened**.

What should Charlie choose to do?

Should Charlie:

a wear his scary vampire mask?

b hide in the toilet?

C show the dentist how well he can clean his teeth?

Charlie, choose **C**

It's normal to be **nervous** of something new. Visits to the dentist aren't too bad and they help to make sure your teeth stay healthy. The dentist might even give you a sticker, too!

What would YOU choose to do?

Be a big brother, Charlie

Charlie's Mum has a new baby.

Charlie is **jealous**. What if Mum likes the baby more than him?

What should Charlie choose to do?

Should Charlie:

a tell Mum he's worried that she won't love him as much as his new sister?

b try to sell the baby to someone else?

for sale

c be naughty so Mum doesn't ignore him?

Charlie, choose

Mums have lots and lots of love – enough to share between everyone! And Mum will be so **proud** if Charlie helps to look after his new baby sister. It might even be fun!

What would **YOU** choose to do?

Tell someone, Charlie

Charlie doesn't **like** Megan.

She teases him when he walks home from school.

What should Charlie choose to do?

Should Charlie:

a hit Megan?

b tell his teacher or his Mum or Dad?

c hide behind the bushes until Megan has gone?

Charlie, choose **b**

Being brave doesn't always mean doing things on your own. Sometimes, you need a grown-up who knows what to do next. Be brave and tell someone who you trust that you are being picked on.

What would YOU choose to do?

Well done, Charlie!

Hey, look at Charlie! Now he can make all the brave choices, he's feeling much **happier**.

Did you choose the right thing to do? If you did, big cheers for you!

If you chose some of the other answers, try to think about Charlie's choices to help you be brave from now on. Then it will be big smiles all round!

And remember – keep your chin up, just like Charlie!

How to use this book

This book can be used by a grown-up and a child together. It is based on common situations that might make any child nervous or frightened. Invite your child to talk about each of the choices. Ask questions such as 'Why do you think Charlie should play football with Sam?'.

Discuss the wrong choices, as well as the right ones, with your child. Describe what is happening in the following pictures and talk about what the wrong and right choices might be.

- Don't avoid a scary situation. It's easy to miss out on fun if you do.

- Don't use violence when you are frightened.

● Talk to a grown-up about being scared. Don't be naughty just to get their attention.

● Hiding doesn't help. The scary thing won't go away!

Talk about the things people can do to stay brave. They might look for a new friend if they are doing something they've never done before. They could practise a situation at home using role play. They could make a list of grown-ups they can trust if they need to talk about being scared.

Most of all, try to listen to your child's fears. Never brush off their worries. Children can feel silly for being scared, so let them know that most people get frightened sometimes. Everyone has to learn how to get past that fear. Be brave together!

Glossary

check-up   when the dentist checks your teeth to make sure they are healthy

friendly   talking to other people and letting them join in with your fun

invited   to be asked by someone to go somewhere or do something with them

jealous   wanting what someone else has

nervous   worried or frightened

proud   feeling very pleased with yourself or with someone else

shy   feeling worried about talking to other people

sleepover   to stay overnight at someone's house

Index

Titles in the series

ISBN: 978 0 7502 6644 4

Like all children, Carlos sometimes does things that are wrong, and doesn't come clean. He has lots of choices to make – but which are the TRUTHFUL ones?

ISBN: 978 0 7502 6642 0

Like all children, Charlie sometimes feels a little scared. He has lots of choices to make – but which are the BRAVE ones?

ISBN: 978 0 7502 6645 1

Like all children, Gertie sometimes plays a little dirty. We put Gertie on the spot with some tricky problems and ask her to decide what is FAIR!

ISBN: 978 0 7502 6643 7

Like all children, Harry sometimes takes things that don't belong to him. He has lots of choices to make – but which are the HONEST ones?